My First Reading - Coloring Book

English - Arabic

The builder man has gone to work on a project.

.وقد ذهب الرجل بانى للعمل فى المشروع

The man has bought a shiny new hammer.

.لقد اشترى الرجل مطرقة جديدة لامعة

The man has an ancient hammer.

.الرجل لديه مطرقة قديمة

There is jam on the bread.

هناك مربى على الخبز.

You can put jam on toast to give it more taste.

يمكنك وضع المربى على الخبز المحمص لإضفاء المزيد من الطعم عليه.

Mom bought a new bottle of jam.

اشترى أمي زجاجة جديدة من المربى.

The happy and excited eight is holding up eight fingers

ثمانية سعيدة ومتحمس يحمل ما يصل ثمانية أصابع

The eight is licking its lip because it sees eight trays of fried chicken.

الثمانية تلعق الشفاه لأنها ترى ثماني صواني من الدجاج المقلي.

A spider has eight legs.

العنكبوت لديه ثمانية أرجل.

The white sheep have a lot of fluffy white wool to give away.

.الأغنام البيضاء لديها الكثير من الصوف الأبيض الناعم لتتخلى عنه

This sheep is so fluffy.

.هذه الأغنام رقيق جدا

The sheep are skinny.

.الخراف نحيفة

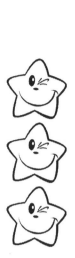

A little cow is walking around near the barn.

بقرة صغيرة يتجول بالقرب من الحظيرة.

The calf is wandering around.

العجل يتجول.

That is a baby cow.

هذا هو البقرة الطفل.

The cereal box got a magician set for Christmas.

حصل صندوق الحبوب على ساحر لعيد الميلاد.

The boy got a wizard action figure for his birthday.

حصل الفتى على شخصية مثيرة في عيد ميلاده.

The book has a wand.

الكتاب له عصا.

An astronaut has to explore our universe so that we would have more knowledge.

.يتعين على رائد فضاء استكشاف عالمنا حتى يكون لدينا المزيد من المعرفة

The astronaut saw something in the distance.

.رأى رائد الفضاء شيئاً ما على بعد

The astronaut is going on a mission.

.رائد الفضاء يجري في مهمة

I have a lot of brushes and pencils.

لِدي الكثير من الفرش والأقلام.

The writing utensils are in the tin can.

أواني الكتابة في العلبة.

I have a lot of pencils.

لِدي الكثير من أقلام الرصاص.

The farmer is driving his truck.

المزارع يقود شاحنته.

The farmer is driving a tractor.

المزارع يقود جرار.

The farmer is chewing on a piece of wheat.

المزارع يمضغ قطعة من القمح.

The postman is giving out the mail in the early morning.

ساعي البريد هو إعطاء البريد في الصباح الباكر.

The postman is delivering mails at the crack of dawn.

ساعي البريد هو تسليم رسائل في صدع الفجر.

The man has a hat.

الرجل لديه قبعة.

The octopus has eight tentacles.

الأخطبوط لديه ثمانية مخالب.

The octopus has very long tentacles.

الأخطبوط لديه مخالب طويلة جدا.

The octopus lives underwater.

الأخطبوط يعيش تحت الماء.

The happy frog is wearing a green hat.

الضفدع السعيد يرتدي قبعة خضراء.

The green frog is wearing a green hat.

يرتدي الضفدع الأخضر قبعة خضراء.

The frog is going to a party.

الضفدع يذهب إلى حفلة.

The snake is licking its lip because it is hungry.

الأفعى تلعق شفتها لأنها جائعة.

The snake is very slimy.

الأفعى عروي جدا.

The snake has polka dots.

الثعبان لديه نقاط البولكا.

Teddy is licking a red and white candy cane.

.تِيدي هي لعَقَ حلوى قَصب حمراء وبيضاء

The brown teddy bear is wearing a bright green hat.

.يرتدي دمية دب بنى قَبعة خضراء زاهية

The bear likes to eat sweets.

.الدب يحب أكل الحلويات

The animals are happy being together again.

الحيوانات سعيدة بالتواجد معًا مرة أخرى.

The animals are having a giant sleepover.

الحيوانات لها النوم العميق.

There are a lot of animals.

هناك الكثير من الحيوانات.

Rabbit thinks that the juicy orange carrot looks yummy.

.الأرنب يعتقد أن الجزر البرتقالي العصير يبدو لذيذ

The bunny is bringing a giant carrot to its family for dinner.

.الارنب هو جلب الجزر العملاقة لعائلتها لتناول العشاء

The bunny likes to eat carrots.

.الارنب يحب أكل الجزر

The frog is trying to catch the fly.

الضفدع يحاول الإمساك بالذبابة.

The frog uses its tongue to catch prey.

يستخدم الضفدع لسانه للقبض على الفرائس.

The frog is hopping.

الضفدع هو التنقل.

The lion is big.

الأسد كبير.

The lion is chasing its tail.

الأسد يطارد ذيله.

The lion is timid.

الأسد خجول.

The number "six" is saying 1+5=6.

الرقَم "ستة" يقول 1 + 5 = 6.

The six are excitedly jumping up and down.

الستة يقفزون بحماس لأعلى ولأسفل.

A butterfly has six legs.

فراشة لها ستة أرجل.

Mr. Snowman is holding a broom and saying goodbye.

السيد Snowman وداعا وقال مكنسة يحمل.

The snowman was just done cleaning the yard.

الرجل الثلجي قد انتهى للتو من تنظيف الفناء.

I made a snowman.

لقد صنعت ثلج.

The dog is playing with a bone.

الكلب يلعب بعظم.

The dog likes to lick the bone.

الكلب يحب لعق العظام.

The dog likes to play.

الكلب يحب اللعب.

The turtle has a robust shell but is very slow.

السلحفاة لديه قذيفة قوية ولكنها بطيئة جدا.

The tortoise lives on land, unlike turtles.

تعيش السلحفاة على الأرض ، بخلاف السلاحف.

The tortoise has a pointy shell.

السلحفاة لديه قذيفة مدبب.

My mom loves to drink tea.

أمى تحب شرب الشاي.

The teapot is short and spout.

إبريق الشاي قصير وصبور.

The teapot has green tea in it.

يحتوي إبريق الشاي على الشاي الأخضر.

The one and the zero are holding hands.

واحد والصفر يدا بيد.

One and Zero together are ten.

واحد والصفر معا عشرة.

I have ten toes in total.

لدي عشرة أصابع في المجموع.

The small cow has orange hair on the top of its head.

البقرة الصغيرة لديها شعر برتقالي على رأسها.

The little cow will eventually be a big one.

البقرة الصغيرة ستكون في النهاية واحدة كبيرة.

The young calf is walking in the field.

العجل الصغير يسير في الحقل.

The cat is taking a nap.

القط يأخذ غفوة.

The cat is very sleepy.

القط نعسان جدا.

The cat is very tired.

القط متعب جدا.

The dragon is waving his hand.

التنين يلوح بيده.

The big ancient dragon says hello to you.

التنين القديم الكبير يقول مرحبا لك.

Dragons are very friendly and have scales on their backs.

التنين ودية للغاية ولها جداول على ظهورهم.

We use the umbrella when it's raining.

.ستخدم المظلة عندما تمطر

The umbrella shelters you.

.المظلة مأوى لك

It's raining.

.انها تمطر

My dad works on the computer.

والدي يعمل على الكمبيوتر.

The laptop is saying hi to the user.

الكمبيوتر المحمول يقول مرحبا للمستخدم.

That is my dad's computer.

هذا هو جهاز كمبيوتر والدي.

The Easter Bunny is painting a chocolate egg.

.الأرنب عيد الفصح هو رسم بيضة الشوكولاته

The Easter Bunny likes to paint eggs.

يحب عيد الفصح لرسم البيض

The rabbit is entering an egg painting contest.

.الأرنب يدخل مسابقة الرسم على البيض

The goat is eating grass.

الماعز يأكل العشب.

The goat is grazing in the meadow.

الماعز ترعى في المرج.

The goat is sleepily walking around.

الماعز يتجول في النعاس.

I love to drink strawberry juice.

.أنا أحب أن أشرب عصير الفراولة

The strawberry is drinking cold refreshing juice.

.الفراولة تشرب عصير منعش بارد

The strawberry is red.

.الفراولة حمراء

The number "two" is holding up bunny ears.

.الرقَم "اثنان" يحمل آذان الأرنب

Number two is posing for a selfie.

.رقَم اثنين هو يطرح لالتقاط صورة شخصية

I have two ears.

.لدي آذان

HO HO HO!

Santa is having fun.

.سانتا يلهون

Santa Claus is laughing at a hilarious joke.

.سانتا كلوز يضحك على مزحة فرحان

Santa is fat.

.سانتا سمين

The little boy was running.

الولد الصغير كان يركض.

The sprinter is winning first place in a race.

العداء يفوز بالمركز الأول في السباق.

The boy is running.

الولد يركض.

Santa Claus is giving extraordinary presents to excited kids.

سانتا كلوز هو تقديم هدايا غير عادية للأطفال متحمس.

Santa Claus is delivering presents to the children.

سانتا كلوز يسلم الهدايا للأطفال.

Santa is happy.

سانتا سعيد.

The xylophone is an instrument like the piano.

.إكسيليفون هو أداة مثل البيانو

The xylophone is a very cool instrument.

.إكسيليفون أداة رائعة جدًا

The xylophone is a colorful instrument.

.إكسيليفون هو أداة ملونة

An owl is teaching the kids in school about work.

البومة تقوم بتعليم الأطفال في المدرسة عن العمل.

Mr.Owl teaches the 3rd grade.

يعلم الصف الثالث Mr.Owl.

The owl is a language arts teacher.

البومة هو مدرس فنون اللغة.

The zebra has black and white stripes.

.حمار وحشي لديه خطوط سوداء وبيضاء

The zebra is smiling widely

حمار وحشي يبتسم على نطاق واسع

The zebra has a tail.

.حمار وحشي لديه ذيل

The Chipmunk is about to eat a brown acorn.

السنجاب على وشك أكل بلوط بني.

The chipmunk brought home a giant acorn.

جلب السنجاب المنزل بلوط عملاق.

The chipmunk has a soft tummy.

السنجاب لديه البطن لينة.

Santa is lugging a large brown bag of gifts to his sley.

سانتا يجلب حقيبة كبيرة من الهدايا البني لبذخه.

Santa Claus is carrying a leather bag filled with gifts.

سانتا كلوز يحمل حقيبة جلدية مليئة بالهدايا.

Santa is going to give out presents.

سانتا سوف تعطيه الهدايا.

The rabbit goes out to buy more orange carrots.

يخرج الأرنب لشراء المزيد من الجزر البرتقالي.

The rabbit just plucked some carrots out of the garden.

التقط الأرنب بعض الجزر من الحديقة.

The Easter Bunny is going to give out chocolate eggs.

سوف عيد الفصح الأرنب إعطاء البيض الشوكولاته.

The rabbit is thinking about something.

.الأرنب يفكر في شيء

The rabbit is confused.

.الارنب مرتبك

The rabbit has long ears.

.الأرنب له آذان طويلة

The bat is ready to fly.

الخفافيش جاهز للطيران.

The bat is hugging the letter.

الخفافيش يعانق الرسالة.

The bat sleeps upside down.

الخفافيش ينام رأسا على عقب.

The elephant is shy.

الفيل خجول.

The elephant has big ears.

الفيل له آذان كبيرة.

The elephant has eyelashes.

الفيل لديه رموش.

The elephant has a long trunk to spray water.

الفيل لديه جذع طويل لرش الماء.

The elephant has a long trunk.

الفيل لديه جذع طويل.

The elephant lives in the zoo.

الفيل يعيش في حديقة الحيوان.

The chicken is saying hello to us.

الدجاج يقول مرحبا لنا.

The white chicken is wearing an artist's hat.

الدجاج الأبيض يرتدي قبعة فنان.

The rooster has a big beak.

الديك لديه منقار كبير.

The maid is cleaning our room.

الخادمة تقوم بتنظيف غرفتنا.

The little girl is carrying two buckets loads of water.

الفتاة الصغيرة تحمل دلوين من الماء.

The girl is wearing a dress.

الفتاة ترتدي الفستان.

The number "five" is trying to give you a high five.

الرقَم "خمسة" يحاول أن يعطيك خمسة عالية.

The five are saying its name out loud, so others will know.

يقول الخمسة اسمها بصوت عالٍ ، حتى يعلم الآخرون.

I have five fingers on 1 of my hands.

لدي خمسة أصابع على يدي.

The smiling number nine is saying its name out loud.

رقَم تسعة يبتسم يقول بصوت عالٍ.

The nine is saying that 4+5=9.

يقول تسعة أن 4 + 5 = 9.

My sister has nine stuffed animals.

أختي لديها تسعة حيوانات محشوة.

Ram has a large horn and fluffy wool.

رام لديه قرن كبير وصوف رقيق.

The ram is smiling because it just took a bath.

الكبش يبتسم لأنه استغرق حمامًا.

This ram lives in the farmhouse.

يعيش هذا الكبش في المزرعة.

My cat likes to eat fish.

قَطَتِي تحب أكل السمك.

The cat is looking for more treats.

القط يبحث عن مزيد من بعامل.

My cat has big eyes.

قَطَتِي لها عيون كبيرة.

The children are going on a field trip on the yellow bus.

.الأطفال ذاهبون في رحلة ميدانية على الحافلة الصفراء

The children go to school on a bus.

.يذهب الأطفال إلى المدرسة على متن حافلة

The kids on the school bus are going to school.

.الأطفال في الحافلة المدرسية ذاهبون إلى المدرسة

Happy Teddy is opening his box of presents from Santa.

سعيد تيدي يفتح صندوقه من الهدايا من سانتا.

The teddy bear is opening his second present.

الدب تيدي يفتح له هدية ثانية.

The bear has a present.

الدب لديه هدية.

The one is saying its name.

واحد يقول اسمه.

Number one got first place at a competition.

رقم واحد حصل على المركز الأول في المنافسة.

I have one nose.

لدي أنف واحد.

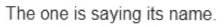

That boy works in a band and plays the drum.

هذا الفتى يعمل في فرقة ويلعب الطبل.

The drummer is leading a huge costume parade.

لاعب الدرامز يقود موكب ضخم للأزياء.

He looks joyful.

إنه يبدو بهيجة.

The animals are having a big celebration.

الحيوانات لها احتفال كبير.

The animals invited the monkey and the parrot to join their sleepover.

دعت الحيوانات القرد والببغاء للانضمام إلى النوم.

I went to the zoo.

ذهبت إلى حديقة الحيوان.

That is a beautiful ring.

هذه حلقة جميلة.

The ring has a diamond jewel on it.

الحلبة لديها جوهرة الماس على ذلك.

That is my ring.

هذا هو حلقتي.

The gardener is going to plant flowers

البستاني سوف يزرع الزهور

The gardener is going to plant some seeds.

البستاني سوف يزرع بعض البذور.

The farmer has a beard.

المزارع لديه لحية.

The cute monster is flying around.

الوحش لطيف تحلق حولها.

The monster has a pointy horn.

الوحش لديه قَرن مدبب.

The little monster has a long tail.

الوحش الصغير له ذيل طويل.

The giraffe has an extremely long neck.

الزرافة لها عنق طويل للغاية.

The giraffe has many spots.

الزرافة لديها العديد من المواقع.

The giraffe eats vegetables.

الزرافة تأكل الخضار.

The engineer is holding a wrench.

المهندس يحمل وجع.

The engineer is going to fix a fancy blue car.

سيقوم المهندس بإصلاح سيارة زرقاء فاخرة.

He has a suitcase.

لديه حقيبة

A smart owl is reading an alphabet book.

بومة ذكية تقرأ كتاب الأبجدية.

The young brown owl is learning to read.

البومة البنية الصغيرة تتعلّم القراءة.

Owl likes to read big books.

البومة يحب قراءة الكتب الكبيرة.

My mom bought me a new backpack to take to school.

.اشترتني أمي حقيبة ظهر جديدة لأخذها إلى المدرسة

The green backpack is holding all my belongings.

.حقيبة الظهر الخضراء تحتفظ بكل متعلقاتي

My bag has many pockets.

.حقيبتي لديها العديد من الجيوب

The kite is on the ground.

الطائرة الورقِية على الأرض.

The kite is on the ground.

الطائرة الورقِية على الأرض.

The kite has a beautiful tail.

الطائرة الورقِية لها ذيل جميل.

The magician plays a trick.

.الساحر يلعب خدعة

The magician summoned a rabbit out of his hat.

.استدعى الساحر أرنبًا من قبعته

The rabbit is very young.

.الأرنب صغير جدا

The letter N stands for a nose.

الحرف N الألف على لتقف.

The nose is used for smelling things.

يِستخدم الألف في شم الأشياء.

The nose is breathing.

الألف يِتنفس.

The frog is waving to us.

الضفدع يلوح لنا.

The frog says goodbye to me and you.

الضفدع يقول وداعا لي ولكم.

The frog has a big mouth.

الضفدع لديه فم كبير.

The duck has a big nose.

البطة لها أنف كبير.

The duck just dropped its little oval eggs.

البطة فقط أسقطت بيضاها البيضاوي الصغير.

The duck has three eggs.

البطة لديها ثلاث بيضات.

The Pencil is leaving to go on a long relaxing vacation.

يغادر قلم الرصاص للذهاب في عطلة طويلة الاسترخاء.

The pencil wakes up bright and early to go to work.

يستيقظ قلم رصاص مشرقًا ومبكراً للذهاب إلى العمل.

The pencil put on a big smile and went to work.

وضع القلم على ابتسامة كبيرة وذهب للعمل.

The dragon just ate something spicy, so he needed water.

.كان التنين يأكل شيئًا حارًا ، لذا فهو بحاجة إلى الماء

The dragon is very thirsty.

.التنين عطشان جدا

The dragon is sick.

.التنين مريض

The policeman is mad.

الشرطي مجنون.

The policeman is angry at some rotten teenagers.

الشرطي غاضب من بعض المراهقين الفاسدين.

He is wearing sunglasses.

يرتدي نظارة شمسية

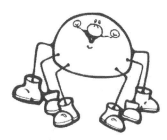

The crocodile is excited.

تمساح متحمس.

The jumping crocodile is happy.

تمساح القفز سعيد.

The alligator is jumping.

التمساح يقفز.

Chef Octopus is serving a delicious turkey dinner.

يقدم الشيف الأخطبوط عشاء الديك الرومي اللذيذ.

The octopus cooked delicious food for its friends.

الأخطبوط طهى الطعام لذيذ لأصدقائه.

The octopus is working as a chef and serving food.

الأخطبوط يعمل طاهيا ويقدم الطعام.

A violin can play beautiful music if played correctly.

يمكن للكمان تشغيل الموسيقى الجميلة إذا تم تشغيلها بشكل صحيح.

The violin is one of the most fantastic instruments.

الكمان هو واحد من أكثر الأدوات الرائعة.

The violin is a musical instrument.

الكمان هو آلة موسيقية.

Funny, Mr. Clown is giving away colorful balloons.

.مضحك ، السيد مهرج هو التخلي عن البالونات الملونة

The clown is holding three colorful balloons.

.المهرج يحمل ثلاثة بالونات ملونة

The clown likes to give out balloons to little kids.

يحب المهرج إعطاء البالونات للأطفال الصغار

This dog is wagging its tail for more treats.

.هذا الكلب هو يهز ذيله لمزيد من يعامل

The dog has a golden collar.

.الكلب لديه طوق ذهبي

That is a fat dog!

إهذا كلب سمين

The green parrot came from the forest to the zoo.

جاء الببغاء الأخضر من الغابة إلى حديقة الحيوان.

The parrot is just learning how to fly in the sky.

الببغاء هو مجرد تعلم كيفية الطيران في السماء.

The parrot is colorful.

الببغاء ملون.

He likes to paint.

يحب الطلاء.

The house painter is almost done with his daily work.

يكاد يكون الرسام المنزل مع عمله اليومى.

He has a bucket of paint.

لديه دلو من الطلاء.

The boy is late for school, so he is sprinting.

الفتى متأخر للمدرسة ، لذلك فهو يركض.

The boy is preparing for school.

الصبي يستعد للمدرسة.

The boy is excited to go to school.

الولد متحمس للذهاب إلى المدرسة.

The old goat is proud of its golden bell.

الماعز القديم فخورة بالجرس الذهبي.

The goat has four hooves.

الماعز لديه أربعة حوافر.

The goat has a friend.

الماعز لديه صديق.

I had a small birthday cake for my party.

كان لدي كعكة عيد ميلاد صغيرة لحزبي.

This birthday cake is for a little kids.

كعكة عيد الميلاد هذه للطفل الصغير.

I have a candle on my cake.

لدي شمعة على كعكة بلدي.

The iguana is hiding behind the letter I.

.الإعوانا تختبئ خلف الحرف الأول

The iguana is curling around the alphabet.

.الإعوانا تتجعد حول الأبجدية

The iguana has a long tail.

.الإعوانا لديه ذيل طويل

The hippo has a big head.

.فرس النهر لديه رأس كبير

The hippo is amazed at how big his teeth are.

.فاجأ فرس النهر في حجم أسنانه

The hippo has a big head.

.فرس النهر لديه رأس كبير

The delivery man sent us a package.

أرسل رجل التسليم لنا حزمة.

The workman is towing some heavy boxes.

العامل يسحب بعض الصناديق الثقيلة.

He is sleepy.

إنه نعسان.

The boy is carrying so many books!

الصبي يحمل الكثير من الكتب!

The smart little boy is carrying heavy books to study.

الولد الصغير الذكي يحمل كتباً ثقيلة للدراسة.

The boy is carrying a lot of books.

الصبي يحمل الكثير من الكتب.

The chef serves delicious-looking food.

يقدم الطاهى الطعام اللذيذ.

The chef made yummy pasta for everyone to share.

جعل الشيف المعكرونة لذيذ للجميع للمشاركة.

The chef has a napkin.

الشيف لديه منديل.

The dragon is using the rock to build its house.

يستخدم التنين الصخرة لبناء منزله.

The dinosaur is getting a plate for his food.

الديناصور هو الحصول على طبق لطعامه.

The dinosaur has a pillow.

ديناصور لديه وسادة.

My duck, stuffed animal, is wearing a hat.

بطي ، حيوان محشو ، يرتدي قبعة.

The little duck is very squeaky.

بطة صغيرة صار جدا.

The toy duck has webbed feet.

وقد بطة لعبة قدم مكنف.

The chick is on the telephone talking with his friend.

الفرخ على الهاتف يتحدث مع صديقه.

The little chick is using his mother's phone to play music.

يستخدم الفرخ الصغير هاتف والدته لتشغيل الموسيقى.

The bird is small.

الطائر صغير.

The ladybug is on the leaf.

الخنفساء على ورقة.

The ladybug is smiling.

الخنفساء تبتسم.

The ladybug has six legs.

الخنفساء لديها ستة أرجل.

The red and black ladybug is just done eating some leaves.

‫يتم الخنفساء الأحمر والأسود فقط تناول بعض الأوراق.‬

The ladybug is eating a piece of lettuce.

‫الخنفساء تأكل قطعة من الخس.‬

The ladybug has many spots.

‫الخنفساء لديها العديد من المواقع.‬

The number "three" is saying you got 3 out of 3.

الرقَم "ثلاثة" يقول أنك حصلت على 3 من 3.

Number three is counting to three.

رقَم ثلاثة هو العد لثلاثة.

I have three buttons on my dress.

لدي ثلاثة أزرار على ثوبي.

Talented, Mr. Clown is juggling five red balls.

.موهوب ، السيد مهرج هو شعوذة خمس كرات حمراء

The funny clown is juggling with skill.

.المهرج مضحك هو شعوذة مع المهارة

The clown is juggling balls for his performance.

.المهرج هو شعوذة كرات لأدائه

The bee is wearing a pink pacifier to calm itself.

النحلة ترتدي مصاصة وردية لتهدئة نفسها.

The baby bees have very tiny wings.

النحل الصغير له أجنحة صغيرة جدًا.

The baby bee has yellow and black stripes.

نحلة الطفل لديها خطوط صفراء وسوداء.

The wizard likes to work with magic.

يِحب المعالج العمل مع السحر.

The wizard is going to summon a great big dragon.

سيقوم المعالج باستدعاء تنين كبير.

The magician has a wand.

الساحر لديه عصا.

The queen bee has a beautiful wand.

.ملكة النحل لها عصا جميلة

The beehive has a leader who is a magical bee.

.خلية النحل لديه زعيم وهو نحلة سحرية

She is wearing a crown.

.هي ترتدي التاج

A rat is on top of the letter M

فأر في أعلى الرسالة م

The mouse has very long whiskers.

الماوس لديه شعيرات طويلة جدا.

I like mice.

أنا أحب الفئران.

My toy box contains a lot of toys.

.صندوق لعبتي يحتوي على الكثير من الألعاب

The toy chest is full of toys.

.لعبة الصدر مليئة بالألعاب

I have stuffed animals, balls, and other toys in my toy box.

.لدي حيوانات محشوة وكرات وألعاب أخرى في صندوق ألعابي

The rooster is on the fence.

الديك على السياج.

The rooster is waking up everybody.

الديك يستيقظ الجميع.

The rooster is going to wake people up.

الديك سوف يستيقظ الناس.

He is playing a lively tune on his flute.

إنه يلعب لحن حية على الفلوت له.

The boy is practicing the flute to be ready at school.

يمارس الصبي الناي ليكون جاهزًا في المدرسة.

He is a musician.

هو موسيقي.

He is driving a big icecream truck.

إنه يقود شاحنة جيلاتي كبيرة.

The ice cream truck is playing a beautiful song.

شاحنة الآيس كريم تلعب أغنية جميلة.

Come on! The ice cream truck is here!

اهيا! شاحنة الآيس كريم هنا

He is going to work with his suitcase.

هو ذاهب للعمل مع حقيبته.

The businessman is calling his boss.

رجل الأعمال يدعو رئيسه.

He has a walkie talkie.

لديه اسلكية تخاطب.

The waiter is serving juice.

يقدم النادل العصير.

The waiter is serving fresh lemonade to a family.

يقدم النادل عصير الليمون الطازج لعائلة.

He is wearing a bowtie.

إنه يرتدي ربطة.

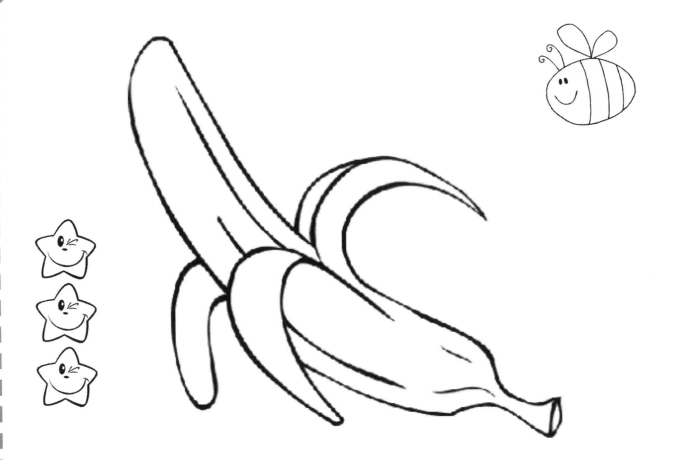

My favorite fruit to eat is a banana.

.فواكهي المفضلة لتداول الطعام هي موزة

The banana is yellow.

.الموز أصفر

My dad bought a lot of bananas in the market.

.اشترى والدي الكثير من الموز في السوق

Santa gave reindeer a big present.

.أعطى سانتا الرنة هدية كبيرة

The reindeer is late to give his present to his friends.

.الرنة متأخرة لتقديم هدية لأصدقائه

Reindeer has a scarf.

.الرنة لديها وشاح

The number "zero" is saying, Ok.

الرقَم "صفر" يقول ، حسنًا.

The zero is saying fine by making the okay gesture.

الصفر هو قول جيد عن طريق لفتة بخير.

I have 0 tails.

لدي 0 نيول.

Made in the USA
Coppell, TX
16 November 2021